echoes
of
eternity

Summer Devotions

Hal M. Helms

PARACLETE PRESS
BREWSTER, MASSACHUSETTS

Echoes of Eternity: Summer Devotions

2008 First Printing

ISBN: 978-1-55725-602-7

Unless otherwise designated, Scripture quotations are taken from the King James Version of the Bible.

Scripture quotations designated RSV are from the Revised Standard Version of the Bible, copyright 1946, 1952, 1971 by the Division of Christian Education of the National Council of the Churches of Christ in the USA. Used by permission.

Original Edition cataloged with the Library of Congress as follows:

Library of Congress Cataloging-in-Publication Data

    Echoes of eternity: listening to the Father.
    p. cm.
    ISBN: 1-55725-173-8 (alk. paper)
    1.   Devotional calendars. I. Paraclete Press.

    BV4810.E24   1996
    242'.2—dc20   96-24801
                                           CIP

10 9 8 7 6 5 4 3 2 1

Published by Paraclete Press
Brewster, Massachusetts
www.paracletepress.com
Printed in the United States of America

Preface

In the very early days of the 3D program, the Reverend Hal Helms and I talked at length about the vision of the work of 3D. One specific vision was that God would speak to each one in the program and assist them with their journey. In the years that followed, Hal was the one who wrote the 3D devotional readings with Scriptures on the topics we selected. I have fond memories of sitting with Hal at his desk, sharing my thoughts and my needs and my struggles, and then watching Hal go through the Bible on his desk, locate a passage, and go straight to his typewriter and write the devotional in a wonderful way. And for over 35 years those writings have been at the core of the program that has touched a million lives.

I didn't know then that Hal had a prayer life that was so very vital to his walk with the Lord, and that he had learned the art of listening to the voice of his heavenly Father. Long before journaling became widespread, for years he kept journals of his conversations with God. In 1996, Hal felt that God was directing him to share these writings with Paraclete Press. He asked that if Paraclete chose to publish his journals, we would not use his name. Paraclete did publish the journals, calling them *Echoes of Eternity: Listening to the Father*. However, because we felt it was vital that people know the journals were written by a Christian minister who had a wonderful relationship with God, we asked Hal for permission to use his name. With his characteristic submission to God's leading, Hal consented to let his name be used.

Over the years, more than 60,000 people have read these words and have been helped deeply. Many of those people were members of the 3D program.

Now I want to introduce this little book to the readers of *Your Whole Life*. My prayer is that you will be encouraged and touched by the voice of God as spoken to my dear friend, who is now eternally in the presence of his Father.

Blessings,

echoes of eternity

Summer Devotions

JUNE

Open my ears that I may
hear
   Voices of truth Thou sendest clear;
And while the wave-notes fall on my ear,
   Everything false will disappear;
Silently now I wait for Thee,
   Ready, my God, Thy will to see.
Open my ears, illumine me,
   Spirit divine.

Clara H. Fiske Scott
1841-1897

June First

But to him that worketh not, but believeth on Him that justifieth the ungodly, his faith is counted for righteousness.

Romans 4:5

I am your righteousness—the only righteousness that will ultimately count. *Your* righteousness is always sullied and mixed with unworthy motives. This I accept and cleanse, because of My own mercy.

I call you to rejoice in My righteousness. It is peace and joy. There is no striving or strain in it. It *is*. I know your frame, that it is dust. But I have not despised the work of My hands. I have not turned My back on My redemption. You are part of a redeemed people, and you have been purchased at a great price, because I have set My love on you. Don't try to figure it out. You cannot. Let it humble you in the right way. Let it free you in the right way. Let it lift you up in the right way. Learn to *flow* in My Spirit—casting aside the weights and sins—even the *pride* in your "righteousness." My yoke is still easy and My burden is still light. Ponder what this means.

June Second

Have I been so long a time with you, and yet hast thou not known Me?
John 14:9

Little faith is better than no faith. Little faith in Me is better than great faith in yourself. I do not despise your little faith, but I do mean for it to grow. You have been in this way too long to be content with such a small and shriveled faith. I deserve better! I have not asked you for great human strength and courage. I know your frame and your fearful nature. But I have given you plenty of "faith material" with which to grow a robust faith. Where is the harvest, My child? Where?

June Third

For he knoweth our frame; he remembereth that we are dust.
Psalm 103:14

"Dust thou art and to dust shalt thou return" was spoken only of the physical flesh—the grain of wheat that must fall into the ground. The physical world is passing away and is destined to decay. But My kingdom, My realm is of another kind. Your glimpses of it are meant to reassure you and yes, *lure* you away from this passing-away world. Cling not to the world, My child. Let it fall away in My providential plan, and reach forth to grasp the eternal that will never fail. There is no sorrow in the loss if your heart sees and seeks the better part.

June Fourth

But when he saw the wind boisterous, he was afraid; and beginning to sink, he cried, saying, "Lord, save me." And immediately Jesus stretched forth His hand, and caught him.

Matthew 14:30,31

Come nearer to me, My child, and do not be afraid. As I reached out to Peter when his faith failed and he began to sink in the boisterous sea, so I am reaching out to you. You do not have to fear Me—for My love is greater than your sin.

You still put too much "stock" in what others think of you. Their good or bad opinions mean too much to you. So you take too much delight in the one, and suffer too much pain in the other. I am your Shield and great Reward. I am the Lord who forgives and redeems you. I am He whose love is unchangeable—and I offer you a fellowship deeper and more stable than you have ever known. I can be the crowning experience of your life—if you will come nearer to Me, and not be afraid of Me.

June Fifth

Heal me, O Lord, and I shall be healed; . . . for Thou art my praise.
Jeremiah 17:14

Praise My goodness, My child, in all things. The pain which I allow in your life, as well as the pleasure, is filled with My goodness. By praising My goodness, you extract the sweetness known only to those who love Me.

I have called you to be an instrument of praise. Most of My world is still full of bitterness and complaint. My goodness is ignored or rationalized, and people pass away without claiming the hidden blessing. I call forth instruments of praise. These are souls who can hear and *begin* to recognize the truth—a truth so magnificent, so full of grace, that people find it hard to believe.

Praise opens the heart to receive the truth of My goodness. It is not by reasoning, argument or logic—but by *praise* that this truth will build the temple for My dwelling in your heart. Praise My goodness, My child, in all things.

June Sixth

But I say unto you, Love your enemies, bless them that curse you, do good to them that hate you, and pray for them which despitefully use you and persecute you.

Matthew 5:44

Doubt not that My hand is here. Let no clouds sully the purpose for which I have brought you here. Many souls have been wounded—not yours alone. My mercy and grace are wider than you can know or imagine. The healing streams from My heart will pour forth for those who will receive them. You do not have to worry about that. Only do not doubt—do not delay to be open to what I am doing. Do not miss the blessing I have prepared for you. Remember, my child, these words of Mine: "Pray for those who hate you and for those who despitefully use you." That prayer will protect you from many assaults of your adversary.

June Seventh

I pray for them. I pray not for the world, but for them which Thou hast given Me; for they are thine. And all Mine are Thine, and Thine are Mine; and I am glorified in them.

John 17:9,10

"I am Thine." You have said these words many, many times with no real conviction in your heart of what they meant. You are *beginning* to realize at a new level their awesome truth.

But now, My child, I say to you, "I am thine." This is no one-way relationship, but involves self-giving on both sides. Just as in marriage both must *give* and *receive*—so with our relationship. Before you are ready to say with "blessed assurance" that you are Mine, I had *given* Myself to you. In very truth, "I am thine."

June Eighth

Remember me, O Lord, when thou comest into Thy kingdom.

Luke 23:42

Your prayers are heard, My child, and they are stored up in My heart. Feeble though they are, and woefully imperfect, I do not despise nor reject them. My tender mercies are indeed over all My works, and I know your frame, that you are dust. But remember, My child, that My love is not like man's love. I love not only the brave and the beautiful. My heart goes out to all who truly seek after Me, however haltingly they walk. So keep on learning to pray—by praying. There is a world of wonder waiting to be discovered through prayer.

June Ninth

To the praise of the glory of His grace, where He hath made us accepted in the Beloved.

Ephesians 1:6

My works are mercy. My paths are peace. Your mind is still full of turbulence, because you still long for a false peace. The peace I give is not dependent on the favor or goodwill of others, and you must let go your demand that "they think well of you." For that demand has its own pain and sickness embedded in it.

I call you to My peace—a peace that passes understanding, a peace free from your life-long striving to be accepted by others. Know, My child, that I have accepted you and loved you with an everlasting love. You have not yet accepted My acceptance—and thereby have robbed yourself of much inner rest. Let them rest who hate you. It is not important that others love you. Blessings abound in the path I have chosen for you. My paths are peace, and My works are mercy.

June Tenth

And he said unto me, My grace is sufficient for thee: for My strength is made perfect in weakness.

II Corinthians 12:9

My strength is made perfect in weakness. This is an eternal truth, and you must learn what it means. I am mindful of your weakness, and your life is in My keeping. The days of your life are numbered—known to Me alone. You have seen that I am the repairer of ruins, the builder up of waste places. You do not have to understand "why" nor "how" this happens. What I call you to do is to rejoice in My works, to see and greet them for what they are.

Greater works are yet to unfold. My blessings are not running out, but they are for those who enter the secret place of My dwelling. Enter with Me every day. Guard the sacrifice as Abraham did of old. Be faithful to the end, and I will give you the crown of life.

June Eleventh

But I trust in thee, O Lord; I say, Thou art my God. My times are in Thy hand.

Psalm 31:14,15 (RSV)

I am the Lord in whose Hand are all the future years. Whatever disappointment or delay I allow to come into your plans and hopes, know of very truth that My way is best. I lead you along rough paths and smooth, green valleys and rugged mountains. I lead you toward the homeland I have prepared for you. The disappointments and sorrows are temporary, and they have their place in your pilgrimage. They wean you from false goals and steer you from wrong paths. Be not dismayed at bad tidings, for My eye is upon you and I will not leave nor forsake you.

June Twelfth

As sorrowful, yet always rejoicing; as poor, yet making many rich; as having nothing, and yet possessing all things.

II Corinthians 6:10

You are never nearer to Me than when your heart is overwhelmed with sorrow and uncertainty. You cannot fathom or understand this reality yet, My child, but you *can* accept it. My Spirit is given, not simply to give you times of joy and brightness, but to guide and lead you through the dark places.

Be of good cheer, and let no clouds keep you from embracing My blessings today, however they may come. Hold not back from those who reach out to you—make an extra effort to show your appreciation to them—for My sake. As surely as I am God, I will be with you. Count on it, build on it. I *am* with you always.

June Thirteenth

But God hath revealed them unto us by his Spirit: for the Spirit searcheth all things, yea, the deep things of God.

I Corinthians 2:10

I know your thoughts. Before you speak them, they are altogether known of Me. My Spirit searches the inner self (the inner man) and sees all. Your distractions, My child, are the fruit of your unfocused heart. You do not yet "will one thing" but try to fit many "goals" into your heart. It will not work. No rival can be allowed in the bride's heart if she is to welcome the Bridegroom. Your soul must be "centrified" in Me if you would taste the fullness of My blessing. I have given you a measure of stability—in spite of this unfocused condition. That is My grace. But I ask you to take much more seriously your need to "will one thing"—My will.

June Fourteenth

The Lord thy God in the midst of thee is mighty; He will save, He will rejoice over thee with joy; He will rest in His love; He will joy over thee with singing.

Zephaniah 3:17

My mercy is new every morning in hearts that seek Me. You can pray no better prayer than to entreat My mercy on those you love.

It is not that I *need* your prayers, My child, but that I allow you to participate in the *joy* of My goodness through your prayers. Your belief and your prayers *do* make a difference, for I have made a place for them in My plan.

Go now to your day with the full assurance that your prayer has been heard, and My mercy is renewed.

June Fifteenth

Wherefore, my beloved brethren, let every man be swift to hear, slow to speak, slow to wrath.

James 1:19

My child, My message today is this: watch your thoughts and your speech. They carry the potential of great harm. Be swift to hear and slow to speak—swift to hear any word against you, swift to hear the gentlest rebuke of My Spirit—and slow to speak the impulsive, critical thought that elevates you momentarily in your own eyes.

The race is not to the swift, nor the battle to the strong. Take your eyes off false goals. Let me lead you to the joys of My kingdom, where pride and place *have* no place, and where true rest is found even in the midst of work. That is what I offer you today—*today*—if you will listen to My voice and heed.

June Sixteenth

Thou tellest my wanderings: put Thou my tears in Thy bottle: are they not in Thy book?

Psalm 56:8

You are still a wandering sheep, scurrying about in your mind in various corners of My pasture. You still gaze out over the protective wall I have erected for your safety, and let your mind go after that which I have denied you. This inevitably brings turmoil and confusion when you could be advancing in a tranquil, settled stability. It is natural for lambs and young rams to gambol in playful wandering, but in maturity I expect more—a graver, more serious focus on the eternal verities I have revealed to you in My love. Let My word *dwell* in you richly as you choose to *dwell* in My will.

June Seventeenth

Who can utter the mighty acts of the Lord? Who can show forth all His praise?

Psalm 106:2

Praise My infinite compassion which I have freely bestowed on you. Praise befits the upright. Praise lifts up the spirit. Praise builds up faith. Praise defeats the enemy's stratagems. Praise joins your prayer to heaven, where My saints are already united in unending praise.

Earth's sorrows are but the backdrop against which the glory of My compassion shines. They cannot dim that glory in the heart that is filled with praise. Praise is a weapon too little appreciated and too little used by My people. I have given it as a gift and have long instructed that it be used. There are no obstacles that cannot be overcome. But My ways are not the ways of the world. Worldly wisdom will fail. But praise—true praise and persistent praise in the face of darkness—*will* prevail.

June Eighteenth

For whosoever shall save his life shall lose it; but whosoever shall lose his life for my sake and the Gospel's, the same shall save it.

Mark 8:35

My child, give over your desire to be liked or loved. You are much too easily affected by signs of being slighted. I have told you that I love you with an everlasting love. My love determines what I allow to come into your life. Yes, My *love* determines that, so be at peace and learn to love others with an undemanding, unself-conscious love, which I will give you—if you seek it sincerely and earnestly.

June Nineteenth

Thou art worthy, O Lord, to receive glory and honor and power; for thou hast created all things, and for Thy pleasure they are and were created.

Revelation 4:11

You are held in the Hand that holds the world. You are kept by the Power that rules the universe. I have said, "None can pluck you from My hand." It is not your feelings that keep you. It is not even your faith—for I know that waxes and wanes quickly under differing circumstances. No, it is My hand that holds you, My child, and protects you when you are least aware of it.

When your eyes are open and you are able to see this reality, give thanks and offer praise. When you cannot see or feel the reality, still give thanks and offer praise. That is an act of faith with which I am pleased. And by the exercise of your faith, it will grow stronger and steadier.

June Twentieth

If ye then, being evil, know how to give good gifts unto your children, how much more shall your Father which is in heaven give good things to them that ask Him?

Matthew 7:11

My heart is a free and ever-flowing heart of generous love. I take pleasure in doing good for My children. Beyond mere perfunctory gratitude for My gifts, I seek a relationship of unshakable trust in My goodness. I seek hearts that come to rest in My unfailing goodness. Those hearts cannot be shaken from their sure foundation by any change of circumstances. Circumstances do and must change, but My goodness changes not. This, My child, is what all My blessings and provisions are meant to effect—*your* unshakable faith in My unchanging goodness.

June Twenty–first

Out of Zion, the perfection of beauty, God hath shined.

Psalm 50:2

I take pleasure in providing blessings for My children. The beauty you see and enjoy is a gift of My love. You have a super abundance of it where I have placed and kept you. To enjoy it fully you must accept it as My gift of love. To reap all the benefits I intend, you must surrender your fretting. The earth is Mine and the fullness thereof. Do not lust after what I have denied you, but embrace what I have given so freely. I take pleasure in providing blessings for you, but I am saddened and grieved when you despise them and fail to recognize My fatherly care.

June Twenty–second

Ye ask, and receive not, because ye ask amiss, that ye may consume it upon your lusts.

James 4:3

Desires granted, desires denied—both flow from My sovereign will. You see and recognize My goodness in those I have granted. You do not yet see and recognize *clearly* My goodness in those I have denied. But it is all the same—My goodness at work for your good. It could not be otherwise, My child. Even now, as you wait long-delayed "answers" to your prayers, My work is still going on. Your faith is still weak and unstable. A small set-back throws it into confusion. My goal for you far exceeds what you can think or imagine. So do not spend time and energy mourning the loss of desires denied. Let them go in their time and be replaced by hopes that harmonize with My loving will.

June Twenty–third

And it shall come to pass, that like as I have watched over them, to pluck up, and to break down, and to throw down, and to destroy, and to afflict; so will I watch over them, to build, and to plant, saith the Lord.

Jeremiah 31:28

Yes, you need Me. I am your life, your breath, and you are sustained every moment by My power and My will. Not a sparrow falls without My permission. The world seems to be "out of control." But I have set limits on its freedom, and I keep faithful watch over My own. Yes, the world lies "in the power of the evil one"—through the disobedience and rebellion of My children. The way is still narrow that leads to life, and few there still are who find and follow it. Your little world is a small one, but My Spirit within is ever pushing out the borders to make room for My loving concern to live in you. Let this happen. Let pride and prejudice fall away, and see the beauty and joy of allowing My love to reign where your pettiness and self-righteousness ruled and crippled. Yes, My child, you need Me. I am your life, and will be your greater life—if you will.

June Twenty–fourth

The Lord did not set his love upon you, nor choose you, because you were more in number than any people; for ye were the fewest of all people: But because the Lord loved you.

Deuteronomy 7:7,8

My dear child, My love for you is sovereign and unchangeable. Your love for Me is fickle and erratic. Nevertheless, I tell you, My love is the firm foundation on which all your hope is founded—not your emotions or lack of them. Of My grace I give you to experience the feeling of love—the love My Spirit has shed abroad in your heart. But even when you feel arid and listless, My unchanging love is toward you.

I would have you grow in love and stability against the faithless fear that mars our relationship. You need much healing and deliverance there. It affects your relationships with others—not just with Me. I know your frame. I remember whence you came. I do not despise your beginnings nor reject you for your sins. My love is unchangeable. Let your love build on that.

June Twenty–fifth

The Lord seeth not as man seeth; for man looketh on the outward appearance, but the Lord looketh on the heart.

I Samuel 16:7

I know your heart better than you know it. I am acquainted with all its foibles and failings. I know its dark corners and its supreme concentration on itself. Yet I do not despise your cries and groans for greater stability and light. I have come to aid—to save—not to condemn. I am doing a work within, and you have My solemn, sovereign word: I will complete it. All I ask of you is that you continue to be open to Me, and follow through in obedience to My word. It shall be well with you, that I may be glorified.

June Twenty–sixth

Let us therefore cast off the works of darkness, and let us put on the armor of light.

Romans 13:12

As the light brings life to the earth, so My light brings life to your soul. My light banishes the darkness of hidden sin, the darkness of evil thoughts, the breeding places of soul-sickness and death.

Put away the works of darkness and choose the light-filled way. Let My sun drive out your dark and dank swamps of thought and feeling. Remember, My child, I am the Light of the world. Those who follow Me shall not walk in darkness but have the light of life. Leave the darkness—flee from it and hasten to Me.

June Twenty–seventh

Thou wilt show me the path of life; in Thy presence is fullness of joy; at Thy right hand there are pleasures evermore.

Psalm 16:11

I am your soul's delight. In My presence is *fullness* of joy. I give you, My child, a foretaste of heaven's pleasure when your heart floods with joy and thanksgiving. The road before you is purposely obscure. You do not need the burden of knowing the details. Grace abounds in each hard place, and I am with you in all you face. Keep your eyes on the goal—to finish the race and win the crown. The crown is for all who are faithful, not just a few. Keep listening to Me. That is important. You still have far to go to maintain a listening attitude. Your mind is still too cluttered with opinions and self-will. This is a training process I have brought you to. Be faithful and the fruit of it will be good. Delight in Me. My goodness is ever before you and never runs out.

June Twenty–eighth

And on the Sabbath we went out of the city by a riverside, where prayer was wont to be made.

Acts 16:13

My dear child, I am nearer than you think, more present to your mind and heart than you know. Your longings for unity and harmony are the fruit of My implanting. Let them encourage you to reach out in prayer for others, for prayers do make a difference. The world could be very different if My people had learned to pray. Your world and the world of those you love will be affected by your faithfulness or lack of faithfulness in prayer. The yearning you feel for "connectedness" is but a drawing of My Spirit toward the unity of spirit and harmony of heart which I will for My people. The place of prayer is a trysting place of the Spirit.

June Twenty–ninth

Brethren, I count not myself to have apprehended: but this one thing I do, forgetting those things which are behind, and reaching forth unto those things which are before, I press toward the mark for the prize of the high calling of God in Christ Jesus.

Philippians 3:13,14

This relationship of love has far to go. The distance is still there on your side. I draw near, but you recoil—still unwilling to risk all for the pearl of great price. I see you playing with the toys of jealousy, vanity, place, and pride. It grieves Me that you have learned so little and are still bound to the old feelings, nursing hurts and slights and being obnoxious withal. I have set you aside in many ways, to aid you in this process and show you the better way. As long as you hold on to your desire to "be somebody," you will suffer the inevitable consequences and miss My best for you. Come to Me, My child, and do not draw back. Let Me show My saving, healing power in the likes of you. You have nothing to lose but your pain.

June Thirtieth

Being found in fashion as a man, He humbled Himself and became obedient unto death, even the death of the cross.

Philippians 2:8

Dear to My heart are those who will follow Me in My humiliation. The world can still recognize goodness and self-denial, even though it loves evil and self-assertion. Those who will put down the secret longing to be lifted up in the eyes of others enter into a secret place where I love to abide.

The desire for recognition and appreciation still lives in your heart. I will aid you in mercy as you are willing to receive My aid, in putting this deadly desire to death. It *can* be done—and *will* be done if you are willing. Remember, the *desire* holds you back from Me. What folly, My child, to linger there when I hold out such a prize for you!

JULY

Charles Wesley
1707-1788

From every stormy wind that blows,

From every swelling tide of woes,
There is a calm, a sure retreat:
'Tis found beneath the mercy seat.

There is a scene where spirits blend,
Where friend holds fellowship with friend;
And heaven comes down our souls to greet
And glory crowns the mercy seat.

Talk with us, Lord, Thyself reveal,
While here o'er earth we rove;
Speak to our hearts, and let us feel
The kindling of Thy love.

Here then, my God, vouchsafe to stay,
And bid my heart rejoice;
My bounding heart shall own Thy sway,
And echo to Thy voice.

Thou callest me to seek Thy face,
'Tis all I wish to seek;
To hear the whispers of Thy grace,
And hear Thee inly speak.

July First

For my people have committed two evils: they have forsaken Me, the fountain of living waters, and hewed them out cisterns, broken cisterns, that can hold no water.

Jeremiah 2:13

My dear child, be content with My love. I see your heart still searching for others to love and respect you. Each time you go on such a search you are seeking vanity—emptiness. Do you not know that yet?

It grieves My heart to see My children, to whom I have revealed My mercy and lovingkindness so powerfully and clearly, still go "whoring" after emptiness. And so I ask you again, My child, be *content* with My love. It is enough, and you will come to see that it is more than you can ask or think. But it is seen and felt in its fullness only when you abandon the useless search for that which can never satisfy.

July Second

They shall ask the way to Zion with their faces thitherward, saying, "Come, and let us join ourselves to the Lord in a perpetual covenant that shall not be forgotten."

Jeremiah 50:5

My glory is seen in the mundane—the ordinary paths of the day. Look for Me more faithfully, My child, and you will surely meet Me there. Hidden from your eyes, I watch over you. Unseen, I protect and provide manifold blessings. Unthanked, I still provide.

You would be greatly blessed if you would cultivate and *practice* My presence more faithfully. My presence is there—*with* you. Did I not promise? "Lo, I am with you always, to the close of the age." That was not spoken just to the disciples on the Mount where I left them. It was My word to My people—those who come to Me and follow Me in their hearts. It is for you, My child, it is for you! How weak and foolish you are not to let Me be your constant Companion!

My glory *can* be seen in the ordinary paths. Will you look more faithfully?

July Third

According as He hath chosen us in Him before the foundation of the world, that we should be holy and without blame before Him in love.

Ephesians 1:4

My dear child, I speak to you in love. Your fear of what I might say grows out of an old, sick, and distorted view of Me and My relation to My children. You never ceased to love your own children, and you had no desire that fear of you would remain in that relationship. In like manner, the fear of the Lord is the *beginning* of wisdom, but "perfect love casts out fear." That means that as you mature, your only fear is that of offending or grieving My love—not the self-oriented fear of what I might *do* to you.

I speak to you in love because that is the essence of our relationship, from My perspective. I know that you still have far to go, but I do not despise you nor condemn you for it. Keep growing!

July Fourth

So shall my word be that goeth forth out of my mouth: it shall not return to me void, but it shall accomplish that which I please, and it shall prosper in the thing whereto I sent it.

Isaiah 55:11

I am the Bread of life. My very life is sustenance for your soul. I break the bread of My word, giving you your daily portion, sustaining you in your earthly journey. As the Israelites needed their daily supply of manna, so you *need* My freshly broken Bread.

My word does not return to Me empty. It produces the fruit of the Spirit in your soul. Bury it deeply by faith, so that its fruit may be abundant. I want your life to bear an abundant harvest. Remember, My child, that harvest comes toward the end of the year, and do not mourn that you will not see it all. Trust it to Me, and keep listening for My freshly broken word of life to you. That is more than enough.

July Fifth

For I am the Lord, I change not; therefore ye sons of Jacob are not consumed.

Malachi 3:6

I am with you today, My child, and you have nothing to fear. Go forth in the joy and anticipation of My blessing. Put aside needless worries and thoughts of what might be. They only tangle and crowd the path laid out before you. Be confident and of good courage, for the cause is Mine, not yours. I have promised and I will keep. There is not variableness or changing in Me. You shall yet see My hand at work to bring about My design and desire—so be prepared. Faith is the necessary key to unlock the treasury I have in store. I will help your unbelief if you will stay close to Me in your need.

July Sixth

Incline your ear and come unto me: hear and your soul shall live; and I will make an everlasting covenant with you, even the sure mercies of David.

Isaiah 55:3

Call upon Me and I will answer you. I have said this to you many times. It is enough that I have said it. You can build on that simple word. Call on Me and I will answer you. No one ever called on Me in vain.

Do not fear to come to Me in any condition. Do not let your sin deter your coming. I wait to be merciful. I am the Lord who forgives and heals. Do you not know that *I* know the condition in which you turn to Me? I read the thoughts and intentions of the heart. So do not be afraid of offending Me. Your separation from Me is more harmful than any sin you bring with repentance. Your safety is in staying close to Me.

July Seventh

For the Lord thy God bringeth thee into a good land, a land of brooks of water, of fountains and depths that spring out of valleys and hills.

Deuteronomy 8:7

Drink at the fountain of My love. Long your soul has dwelt in a dry and thirsty land. Drink and be renewed here where living water flows. I am the water of life, the living water that enlivens your dying soul. There can be no life apart from this living water.

I look for abundant growth. I see a soul still shrivelled and dry. I look for abundant fruit. I see but little, and the harvest is nigh. The need is great and the supply is unlimited. The day is still at hand, but night comes, when no man can work. Drink deeply, My child, at the fountain of My love—that your soul may be healed and your fruit may remain.

July Eighth

That they might be unto me for a people, and for a name, and for a praise, and for a glory. . . .

Jeremiah 13:11

Praise is My gift to you. As you lift your heart and voice to join the throngs of the ages, I give back to you far and above anything you can offer to Me. It is part of My sovereign plan that My children are blessed in blessing. When the whole creation shall praise its Creator and Redeemer, healing streams will flow through its veins, to keep it in perpetual health.

There can be no more healing prayer than praise—praise of the whole heart and soul. Praise of the body and voice. You are created as a whole person—and your praise *must* include body, soul, and spirit if it is to be complete. "Out of the mouths of babes Thou hast perfected praise"—why? Because in the simplicity of childhood, they hold nothing back out of "dignity" or "decorum."

My child, *learn* to praise Me more wholly. Praise is My gift to you.

July Ninth

And they heard the voice of the Lord God walking in the garden in the cool of the day; and Adam and his wife hid themselves from the presence of the Lord God amongst the trees of the garden.

Genesis 3:8

Again I tell you, I am the Lord who healeth thee. My promises are still in effect. I see your emotions vacillate between hope and despair. Your *fear* is your enemy. Remember, My child, perfect *love* casts out fear. There is *no* fear in love. I have not forgotten to be gracious. My heart is open to you. Your fear *closes* your heart to Me. You shall yet see the wonder of My grace. I have promised and I will be faithful. I have spoken and I will perform. It is not up to you to bring it about. This is My concern. Only believe! Only trust! Only confess your fear and flee to the Rock!

July Tenth

They looked unto Him, and were lightened; and their faces were not ashamed.

Psalm 34:5

My child, do not hurry. Wait for Me. Let the natural impatience of your soul be put to death by My delay. I know your need. You need not distress yourself. I always come on time. You will learn that if you will continue to wait on Me. I come laden with the gifts you need. Before you call, I am prepared with My answer. Yet your call is necessary, because you need to become needy in your own eyes.

Take your eyes off the circumstances that cause inner turmoil. Leave them to Me. Let My Spirit convict and convert your heart—not out of fear of what others may think or say or do—but in holy sorrow and compunction of heart toward Me. You have yet much to learn about true conviction, deep repentance, and the peace that forgiveness brings.

July Eleventh

One thing have I desired of the Lord, that will I seek after; that I may dwell in the house of the Lord all the days of my life, to behold the beauty of the Lord, and to inquire in His temple.

Psalm 27:4

Out of the deep you have called Me, and out of the deep I have answered you. Deep calleth unto deep. This is where I commune with you, when you turn and truly seek Me. You shall seek Me and find Me *when* you seek Me with all your heart. Deep unto deep.

Yes, you enter into the mystery of the ages, the communion of saints, the anteroom of heaven, when you seek and find Me here. You know the secret joy and strength which they found who have peopled these courts. A day in My courts is better than a thousand elsewhere.

It matters not what the outward surroundings are or were— palace or prison, temple or tabernacle. When My presence is truly sought and found, My glory fills the heart and that is enough.

July Twelfth

And be ye kind to one another, tenderhearted, forgiving one another, even as God for Christ's sake hath forgiven you.

Ephesians 4:32

Come to Me with all your hurts and pain. Know that I the Lord am with you and know each one. You can deal with them in self-pity, deceiving yourself—or you can choose to let them crucify the self-love that demands to be understood and agreed with. Stop defending yourself. As soon as you feel misunderstood—stop. Take a breath and pray to see—really see—the reality of the situation. Whether you are "factually" right or not is not the important thing. The crucial point is to see *into* the situation and take the other's point of view seriously. You often misread this and provoke more conflict and more pain. I will help you, but you must be willing to pay the price—and for you, that is a costly one! But be of good cheer. The end is better than the beginning.

My child, do not fret over the circumstances around you. Do not allow the sin of others to draw you into judgment and self-righteousness. Have mercy on them, as I have had mercy on you. Remember the story of the servant who was forgiven a great debt, but acted unmercifully toward a fellow-servant who owed him a small one. Do not magnify the sin of others in your own mind, but "remember the rock from which you were hewn and the pit from which you were digged." That will enable you to "speak the truth in love" at the appointed time.

July Thirteenth

Surely goodness and mercy shall follow me all the days of my life.

Psalm 23:6

I have magnified My mercy and will magnify it again. Goodness and mercy have followed you all the days of your life, and they shall follow you to the end. But do not presume, My child, on My mercy. Keep watch on the wayward side of your nature which the adversary is ever ready to exploit for his purposes. I do not want to see you hurt by any foolish choice, so My warning is against letting your joy in My mercy make you careless in this area. Being attentive to My presence is your safeguard.

July Fourteenth

The pride of thy heart hath deceived thee.

Obadiah vs. 3

I the Lord your God am speaking to you. Heaven and earth shall pass away—but My love is eternal. My child, you still have far to go and much to receive before the fullness of this truth is in you. You still operate on the basis of merit and punishment—of being good and being bad. You still take pride in the works of My grace, and do not pay the fullness of tribute to Me. The momentary lift you get from such pride comes with a high price. It damages your soul and delays your progress toward maturity. Learn to recognize these feelings and *quickly* bring them to Me before great damage is done, and you find yourself in enemy territory. It can be done. It is not without hope of change, even though your nature is badly bent in this pattern. Credit and glory are not the true fulfillment you have thought them to be. They are chains that bind you to a changing, dying, fickle world. But you *can* break the chains!

July Fifteenth

And let us not be weary in well doing: for in due season we shall reap, if we faint not.

Galatians 6:9

My dear child, wait awhile. Do not be impatient when you do not see an immediate answer to your prayers. Waiting is an important part of the prayer process. It is a great separator of the trivial from the heartfelt request. It is a time for refining of motives in asking. It is an *active* time, not merely an unwanted delay.

Wait awhile. My ears are open to your needs and the needs of those you hold before Me. No prayer is wasted. In My love, I take them into account and turn them to good effect, even when the answer is not what you hoped or wanted. Knowing that secret, pray on—and wait awhile. You will have ample cause to rejoice.

July Sixteenth

And He said, Draw not nigh hither: put off thy shoes from off thy feet, for the place whereon thou standest is holy ground.

Exodus 3:5

In the midst of trouble and uncertainty, I am still your peace. This is the peace that passes all understanding, because it is not tied to nor dependent on the pleasantness of the circumstances of your life. I know the situation you face. I am still Lord of it. What I ask of you is to draw near to Me and stay near to Me "until this storm be overpast." Have I not promised to be with you in trouble? Is My arm shortened that it cannot save? Turn from the fear and unbelief that arise in your heart at the first sign of trouble. Call upon Me and I will answer you. Learn, learn, learn to trust Me—and go forward with Me. Today's Scripture is not there by accident or "coincidence." "Take your shoes off your feet, for the ground on which you stand is holy." That means the *foundation* on which you stand in Me is holy ground. Believe it and do not fear!

July Seventeenth

For all people will walk every one in the name of his god, and we will walk in the name of the Lord our God for ever and ever.

Micah 4:5

Walk in the light that you have, My child, and do not let the darkness draw you away from Me. The way is still narrow and the darkness is still great, but there is light enough on your path. Day will come, but for this time, these shadows remain. *Quit you like a man*, and strive against the enemy and his forces—they war for your soul. You do not have to be strong, but you must stay in the path of light to be safe.

July Eighteenth

I have set before you life and death, blessing and cursing; therefore choose life, that both thou and thy seed may live.

Deuteronomy 30:19

It is all in My hands—your welfare and your future. You are right to rejoice in My mercy, for My mercy is from everlasting to everlasting. Those who taste My mercy have reason to rejoice with exceeding great joy.

My heart is made glad when you begin to move from low thoughts and desires and yearn for heavenly things. I will not force this move on you or anyone, because I have created you with the gift of choice. Choose life, My child, choose life. Choose the higher life—the life I offer you each day, instead of groveling in your own thoughts and desires. Your welfare and your future are in My hands *if* you leave them there. *That* is your "door of hope" in the valley of Achor—an open door. Come through it.

July Nineteenth

Great peace have they which love Thy law; and they shall have no stumbling block.

Psalm 119:165

It is good to wait in My presence. You are being blessed and fed by My Spirit, even when you hear no words. It is good to keep trusting when your prayers are delayed. You have been long in coming to this place, and there is still much ground to reclaim. You have built a fortress around your mind, and trusted in your own thoughts and opinions rather than on Me. They failed you when great need arose, and you were faced with their inability to help. I have not failed you, but you forfeited much peace by your choices. It is good to wait in My presence. This, too, is part of My work to help you regain and reclaim lost ground.

July Twentieth

Honor and majesty are before Him: strength and beauty are in His sanctuary.

Psalm 96:6 (RSV)

The riches of My Word are hidden from the natural eye. It sees the outer "shell" and may even admire what it sees. But to those who are willing to ask, to seek and to knock, My treasury unlocks its greater beauty. Here the soul feasts, and here it finds joys which it cannot describe. Truly, My child, those who find these riches can say, "The lines have fallen to me in pleasant places. I have a goodly heritage." The beauty of holiness is seen and experienced in the garden of love. The glimpses you are given of My beauty and glory are gifts to help you through your hard times. Treasure them and do not forget them.

July Twenty–first

Let us lift up our hearts with our hands unto God in the heavens.

Lamentations 3:41

Lift up your heart! Look to Me and for Me throughout this day. My love does not waver or vacillate. Through the darkest times, My light does not diminish or go out. Only your perception of it changes.

Lift up your heart! Be of good cheer, and do not fear the future. By faith embrace the future as I unfold it. Leave to Me what I design to accomplish with the circumstances you dread. Leave it to Me to turn evil to good. Learn, learn, learn that most important clue to uniting with Me when your understanding is failing you miserably. I will meet you there, and *together* we will walk through the hard places.

Lift up your heart and be of good cheer. My yoke is still easy and My burden is still light.

July Twenty–second

They that sow in tears shall reap in joy.

Psalm 126:5

The early rain and the latter rain—tears given to water the dry ground of your soul. The early rains were the tears that came in your youth, though you were embarrassed by them and did not understand what they were doing. But they opened the ground of your soul to receive impressions of My Spirit and the seed of My Word to grow silently therein. The latter rain is your present gift, again to enable your soul to receive My life-giving Word. Do not despise the tears, and do not try to delve into secrets hidden from you. Let My word grow to bring forth an abundant harvest.

July Twenty–third

But God forbid that I should glory, save in the cross of our Lord Jesus Christ, by whom the world is crucified unto me, and I unto the world.
Galatians 6:14

My child, I will keep you in the cross—in the life-giving sacrifice of My child on Calvary. Mercy flows even yet from that life-giving source. Your life is there, hidden in the mystery of My suffering. Let it break your stony, rebellious heart to know the price I paid for you—yes, My child, for *you*. These are not empty words; these are from your Father's heart.

Let the world pass by with its glory and its shame. Your life—your true life—is here, at the place of sacrifice. Bathe your spirit in the life-giving stream of mercy. Drink from the life-giving stream of mercy. Look deeply into the unfathomable depths of mercy—and let your spirit, your heart, your soul be changed.

July Twenty–fourth

Behold, I stand at the door and knock: if any man hear my voice and open the door, I will come in to him, and will sup with him, and He with me.
Revelation 3:20

My dear child, why is it so hard for you to accept My words of love? Or the reality of My love for you? Have I not proved over and over that I love you with a supernatural and unfailing love? Has My care ever been lacking? Yet you draw back, frightened, guilty, defensive—even against Me.

I will not force Myself beyond that inner citadel. I stand at the door and knock—for My nature is to respect what I have created and given life to. When I said "We will come in and sup with him," I meant that a whole world of friendship awaits those who hear My voice and allow Me free entrance to the inmost recesses. It is Love that stands—that pleads. Let Me take full charge. Don't let pride, fear, jealousy or any shame keep Me from Love's goal. My dear child, why do you think I died for you?

July Twenty–fifth

The blood of Jesus Christ cleanseth us from all sin.

I John 1:7

The wounds of the soul must be cleansed before healing can take place. The cleansing process is painful for you, because the stains are the result of your sinful choices in the past. The more you are aware of this, the easier it makes your cooperation with the process. The light of truth exposes the ugliness of these sores, but the Balm of Gilead then restores lost beauty. Marvel at the goodness that directs My operation, and do not flinch at the necessary pain.

July Twenty–sixth

I will cause the shower to come down in its season; there shall be showers of blessing.

Ezekiel 34:26

I shower upon you the showers of mercy. Forget not all My benefits, My child, for in forgetting you sever yourself from the life-giving water and become arid and fruitless. Abundant grace is always available to you—and remembering prompts you to take hold of it.

My plans for you still move forward. You are not forgotten, and no prayer is prayed in vain when it comes from a repentant, remembering heart. So I bid you again, forget not all My benefits. They are more than the stars in heaven.

July Twenty–seventh

For we have not an high priest which cannot be touched with the feeling of our infirmities; but was in all points tempted like as we are, yet without sin.

Hebrews 4:15

Hidden in the mystery of My love are all the events of your life, good and bad. Have I not said, "As far as the east is from the west, so far have I removed your transgression from Me"? This is not an empty phrase. It is a proclamation of divine mercy to helpless sinners. Forgiveness is the key that unlocks My fulfillment—forgiving those who have wronged or hurt you and *accepting* forgiveness for the wrongs you have committed.

My dear Son entered into the darkest valley of suffering to change the power of guilt into the power of forgiveness. My people know little—almost nothing—of what He accomplished there. Enter into this truth as you have never done and invite others to venture in. In doing so, you enter further into My heart.

July Twenty–eighth

The Spirit searcheth all things, yea, the deep things of God.
                                                                    I Corinthians 2:10

In your dreams I have spoken, and in dark language I have communicated with your spirit. You do not have to understand with your rational mind all that I am doing. You need only to be obedient to that which I clearly speak.

There are depths in the human heart which can be plumbed only by My Spirit. The heart is a deep cavern, and there are many hiding places where sin lurks undetected. The confusions you feel come from these smelly places, and the Spirit seeks them out as you cease resisting Him. "Truth in the inward parts" comes by the Spirit of Truth occupying and enlightening those hidden places.

July Twenty–ninth

And He said unto me, My grace is sufficient for thee: for my strength is made perfect in weakness. Most gladly therefore will I rather glory in my infirmities, that the power of Christ may rest upon me.

II Corinthians 12:9

"My grace is sufficient for you. My strength is made perfect in weakness." Your weakness is a necessary part of our relationship, for your strength would vie with Me if I allowed it to prevail. Your weakness is a gift of safety—to keep you from veering too far from the path of My will. Yes, in years past, My child, your weakness was used to prevent your leaving here. So there is not cause for recrimination against yourself or others—but rather an inner reconciliation between the outer circumstances and inner circumstances of your life.

Rejoice in My grace more and more. It is not an excuse for passivity or sin, but it is a fountain of refreshment and renewal. It is a life-giving cordial, a continuing cause of wonder and gratitude to My children. Since it is *reality*, it cannot lead you astray. I am the God of grace!

July Thirtieth

And after the earthquake a fire; but the Lord was not in the fire: and after the fire a still small voice.

I Kings 19:12 (RSV)

I the Lord your God am with you, My child. Walk this day with Me, consciously seeking to hear and heed "the still small Voice" of My Spirit within your heart. I will speak to you and guide you. Only be careful to listen!

You cannot know the way or the path to follow on your own. Confusion is sown by the adversary to trap the unwary. But I have promised, and My promise is faithful, that I will show the path through the maze.

Your faith will be strengthened if you will be careful to heed My words. You will grow more confident in this new walk, and that is good. I want your faith to become more simple and ready to act. Are you sufficient for this? No, but remember, My child, your sufficiency will be of *Me*. And there is no lack there!

July Thirty–first

The Lord is my light and my salvation; whom shall I fear? the Lord is the strength of my life; of whom shall I be afraid?

Psalm 27:1

Light rises in the dark places when they are opened to My presence. Light dispels the negative and gloomy thoughts and feelings, and scatters the shadows of night. I am the Daystar, the Light-giver who brings hope and gladness to your soul. Welcome Me, My child, with a wide open door—for I come bearing precious gifts. You are not called to dwell in sadness or to pine for those things that cannot be. Let their absences free you to see the wonders I have to unfold before you, and be fully present to them. Trust Me to guide your way, to guard what you have entrusted to Me, to keep you and your loved ones safe from harm—and let My joy be your strength.

AUGUST

Fanny Crosby
1820-1915

Thy Holy Spirit, Lord, alone

Can turn our hearts from sin;
His power alone can sanctify
And keep us pure within.

Thy Holy Spirit, Lord, can bring
The gifts we seek in prayer;
His voice can words of comfort speak
And still each wave of care.

Thy Holy Spirit, Lord, can give
The grace we need this hour;
And while we wait, O Spirit, come
In sanctifying power.

August First

Come unto me, all ye that labor and are heavy laden, and I will give you rest.

Matthew 11:28

I am your Father and your Savior. There is no reason to be cut off from Me. I have called you and I will sustain you to the end. O ye of little faith! How many times have I revealed My tender mercies to you—and yet you fear! Be done with living in the shadows when My light is shining for you. I tell you again: life is to be *lived*, not simply endured. Do not be afraid to reach out, to share your life with others, to extend My blessing to them. I will show you and direct you as you obey. Only *do* live, My child, and learn to trust.

August Second

Jesus said, Have faith in God. What things soever ye desire, when ye pray, believe that ye receive them, and ye shall have them. And when ye stand praying, forgive.

Mark 11:22,24,25

There are no restrictions to limit the extent of your faith in Me. I have not set bounds on what I am able to do in response to the prayer of faith. The limits you put on it are your own, and they do limit the extent and outreach of your prayers. That is a spiritual law which operates for every child of Mine.

Just as muscles atrophy or grow with disuse or use, so faith dwindles or grows with exercise. I seek vigorous, faith-filled children who, like Gideon, in spite of fear, went ahead and dared to trust Me. Your fear restricts, while faith releases. It is a barrier to be overcome if you are to move in the glorious liberty of the children of God. Why wait?

August Third

Exhorting one another: and so much the more, as ye see the day approaching.

Hebrews 10:25

In the early morning light, there is hope for greater light. Shadows flee before the rising sun. Even so, My child, the glimmers of your "early morning light" hold the promise of a clearer day. Shadows of doubt and fear, guilt and sin cannot stand before My light. I am your light and your promise that hope will not be disappointed. You have light enough for every step of today's journey. Rejoice in it, be thankful for it, and you will see that I *am* the Way, the Truth and the Life.

August Fourth

Henceforth there is laid up for me a crown of righteousness, which the Lord, the righteous judge, shall give me at that day; and not to me only, but unto all them also that love His appearing.

II Timothy 4:8

Crowns and honors are Mine to give. They are never to be sought for their own sake. My glory is seen in those who do not seek their own. They are blessed with the secret joy which I impart to the humble. Seek humility, My child, as a treasure more precious than gold. Do not despise the humiliations I send or allow, for they are sharp instruments to prune away the rank overgrowth of pride. Look about you and see the signs that I am at work on your proud nature, to make humility a possibility for you. That is a token of My love.

August Fifth

For evildoers shall be cut off: but those that wait upon the Lord, they shall inherit the earth.

Psalm 37:9

Blessed are those who wait for Me. My coming is always on time, but to you it may seem too long delayed. In the waiting, your desire is tested. I have told you to ask, seek, and knock—to keep on asking, seeking, knocking—for in that process a winnowing is taking place, and the depth of your desire is seen. Distractions offer relief from waiting, so beware the subtlety of their appeal. Fight to stay in focus. I have not abandoned you, and My purpose is still for your good. Remember that always—always, My child. My love for you is an everlasting, eternal love.

August Sixth

He turneth the wilderness into a standing water, and dry ground into watersprings.

Psalm 107:35

My way is in the desert, My child, where hidden springs flow and unexpected oases appear. The desert is the dryness and separateness you feel. You lose sight of the path, you lose sight of the goal of your journey, and you lose sight of the meaning of your days. My oases appear and you are again refreshed, but you cannot stay in that pleasant resting place. My way is in the desert and through the desert—toward your true destination and home. Trudge on, but do not forget your Companion on the way. The journey is not over. The end is not yet.

August Seventh

Take no thought for the morrow: for the morrow shall take thought for the things of itself. Sufficient unto the day is the evil thereof.

Matthew 6:34

Do not worry, do not worry, do not worry! I am He who holds your life in My hand. All is well and shall be well, My child, for I am God. You shall still see My glory revealed, and there *will* be a fulfillment of all I have spoken to you.

August Eighth

In Him was life; and the life was the light of men. And the light shineth in the darkness.

John 1:4,5

Many hues are contained in the sunbeams you see. In like manner, My light contains blessings of many kinds. Some of them you can recognize and enjoy. Others are not visible to your sight or mind, but they work invisibly in the soul to accomplish My purpose. The entrance of My word gives light.

My child, darkness is the absence of light. When darkness threatens your tranquillity, remember that Light dispels darkness—and yours is the responsibility to seek it, and keep on seeking it until the shadows flee before it. You prefer darkness when your heart has turned from Me. Choose light.

August Ninth

The voice of Thy thunder was in the heaven: the lightnings lightened the world: the earth trembled and shook.

Psalm 77:18

My thoughts come to you in the midst of your thoughts. Because you are still bound by your old habits, you do not recognize or greet them. I still choose to speak in the "still, small voice" rather than the thunder. My yoke is easy. I am gentle and lowly of heart. But because I love you and care for your welfare, I *will* speak in thunder if necessary. So tune your heart to hear. Be assured that the Voice is there, and that it *is* possible to commune with Me more consistently than you have ever known.

August Tenth

But the Lord is faithful, who shall establish you, and keep you from evil.
II Thessalonians 3:3

My child, do not fret yourself because of evil doers. They are Mine to deal with, and I am aware of the condition of their hearts.

My mantle of mercy is still over the work of My hands, and you need not fear the evil day. Have I not told you?

I want to see more joy, more faith, more freedom in My children. I want you all to *rejoice* in your salvation which has been achieved at so great a price. As long as you allow fear and foreboding to prevail, you refuse the abundant life I have given you. Obedience and joy must kiss each other. Put off the old garment of doubt and put on the new garment of joy and praise.

August Eleventh

Godliness with contentment is great gain.

I Timothy 6:6

Hear My voice, My child. I speak in the depths. I know your fear and worries, and I am acquainted with your thoughts. Much of your energy is wasted in wounded pride and thwarted dreams. You have not yet fully submitted yourself to My mild yoke, and in your rebellion you have carved a harder one for yourself. Accept My love as I have given it to you. Accept My blessings as I have poured them out on you. Remember that gratitude and grumbling cannot dwell together. Choose which shall reign in the depths of your heart and soul.

August Twelfth

Humble yourselves therefore under the mighty hand of God, that He may exalt you in due time.

I Peter 5:6

Holy, Holy, Holy is the Lord God of Hosts. I dwell in the high and holy place, and seek a dwelling place on earth among the lowly. I am grieved at the ingratitude which allows your heart to close itself from Me. I am merciful and full of compassion, but I am the Holy One. Lose no time in turning to Me, and learn to avoid the ways that lead to darkness and death. You were created for *life*. Embrace My life more fully today, My child.

August Thirteenth

. . . and again I say, Rejoice.

Philippians 4:4

Rejoice, My child, rejoice. Let praise fill your heart and overflow from your life. Believe in the efficacy of prayer—even your own feeble ones. My ear is open even to the sighs of My children. While you wait to see the changes prayer can bring about, rejoice in faith and drive away the scavengers of doubt that would take away your sacrifice of praise. Praise and faith strengthen and nourish one another.

That is why Paul says, "With thanksgiving let your requests be made known to God."

August Fourteenth

They looked unto Him and were lightened, and their faces were not ashamed.

Psalm 34:5

Lift up your hands and your heart to Me and expect My word to be fulfilled. The great sin and barrier to your prayers is your lack of expectant faith. You entertain doubts and accusing thoughts without realizing their true nature and the danger they pose to your welfare. I bid you to believe, but I will not force you to believe. That I have reserved for you. It is a choice, and if you will make it against your fearful thoughts and feelings, you will see its fruit. Leave the hard questions aside, and come as a little child to Me.

August Fifteenth

. . . Christ Jesus came into the world to save sinners, of whom I am chief.

I Timothy 1:15

I am full of truth and grace. The record of the years will testify to My goodness and mercy. My will and intention for you has never changed. It is to bring you out of your fickleness and folly into the likeness of My child. When the task is complete, you will be able to see what is now hidden from your eyes—My mercy at work at all times—even when you were farthest from Me. You still want to take credit, and you still think you are better than others. Pray for courage to face the truth and for gratitude that you have been kept by My sovereign power from yourself.

August Sixteenth

. . . I am He who searcheth the reins and hearts.

Revelation 2:23

Your days are based on anxiety and fear. These in turn are rooted in pride, fear of looking bad to others. My days bring peace. My timetable is always sufficient to accomplish what I require. Let My peace stand guard over your mind, and let your anxious thoughts fade away like the morning dew. O foolish and slow of heart to believe! Have I not always been faithful? Give over the reins, My child, give them over that peace may prevail.

August Seventeenth

But avoid foolish questions, and genealogies, and contentions, and strivings about the law; for they are unprofitable and vain.

Titus 3:9

Take heed and beware of foolish arguments. They foment strife and division of spirit. Restrain your strong, natural impulse to push for your own ideas and opinions. Learn to be quiet. Learn to leave to Me the settling of great questions and small ones. Seek peace and pursue it. In your weakness My strength can and will prevail. In your strength, you nullify Mine. This is an important step which I am offering you, and I will help you if you will heed My word.

August Eighteenth

So great a cloud of witnesses . . .

Hebrews 12:1

My dear child, My mercy-seat is always open to you. Here you are surrounded by many who have frequented it before you. You are not aware of their presence or their aid in your journey, but they are partners with you in the struggle you face.

Be not afraid to embrace new understandings as you journey with Me. New scenes and new occasions have their place in your growth. You are reluctant to give up old ideas and habits, even as you try new ones. You still fear what others will think about you. But remember how steady My mercy has been, and do not fear to widen the scope of your spiritual vision—it is safe here at the mercy-seat.

August Nineteenth

With the merciful Thou wilt show Thyself merciful.

Psalm 18:25

I have this against you, My child, that you show so little mercy to those who need it most. Mercy is not softness nor compromise with truth, but truth without mercy can be hard and sharp. It can build walls when bridges are needed.

As I rehearse the many examples and instances of My mercy to you, remember the parable of the servant who would not forgive the debt of his fellow-servant. Learn from this that I intend My mercy to be multiplied through you to others. Be not deceived nor think of yourself more highly than you ought to think. While there is yet time, ask for guidance and set your heart to learn and practice being a mercy-giver.

August Twentieth

And I will give thee the treasures of darkness, and hidden riches of secret places, that thou mayest know that I, the Lord, which call thee by thy name, am the God of Israel.

Isaiah 45:3

Blessed are those who listen, for they shall hear. Blessed are those who hear, for they shall know. I am known of those who listen and those who heed. My heart is open to those who seek Me, and I never refuse those who come to Me.

I have moved your heart to yearn for Me, and denied you the satisfactions that would have falsely sated your hunger. That thirst you feel for a closer companionship with Me is meant to keep you dissatisfied with anything less. Do not look for full satisfaction here in any earthly relationship or any place. Only in Me, My child, is your true home and goal. Journey on.

August Twenty–first

Lo, I am with you always, even unto the end of the world.

Matthew 28:20

I go before you, My child, and prepare the way. When you walk in My way, your life fulfills My purpose for you. When you follow your own path, the results are dead and lifeless. Redeem the time,

My child. These days have been given for purposes you cannot fully see nor understand. Yours is not to view the distant scene, but to stay close to Me and let My will prevail. That is reward enough for now, and there is much to do.

August Twenty–second

Who forgiveth all thine iniquities; who healeth all thy diseases.
Psalm 103:3

My child, I am still healing ancient wounds in your soul. The process is slow and often hidden from your view. But I tell you, of a truth, it is taking place. You are not marking time and your circumstances are not accidents. So lift up your head and your heart, and receive each day as a gift. You do not know the end, but I do, and I am leading you toward My goal for you.

August Twenty–third

Yea, though I walk through the valley of the shadow of death, I will fear no evil; for Thou art with me.
Psalm 23:4

My dear child, I have no delight in the suffering of My people. I allow it only for their eternal good. Blessed are those who turn to Me in their trouble, for I am a God of mercy and compassion. The valleys through which I call you to go need not frighten you. The shadows and darkness are only for a time. Let your faith grow strong when darkness comes. Faith will overcome where daylight cannot prevail. Suffering purges away the rank growth of self—if you let it do its work. There are two ways in which I turn it to good: by its pruning and by My healing. In both ways I bring blessing to My chosen ones.

August Twenty–fourth

My times are in Thy hand: deliver me from the hand of mine enemies. Save me for Thy mercies' sake.

Psalm 31:15,16

Your prayers are heard, My child, and you need not fear. Hold fast to what you know, to My dealings and the revealings of My heart to you. These are steady lodestars by which to chart your course. You need not fear what lies ahead, because I always prepare the way for you. When you walk with Me, no harm can come to you. The only danger you have to face is your own unstable and unfaithful nature. That requires diligence and a readiness to confront its twists and turns.

August Twenty–fifth

For the Lord God is a sun and shield: the Lord will give grace and glory: no good thing will He withhold from them that walk uprightly.

Psalm 84:11

No good thing have I withheld from you, My child. In My wisdom and mercy, I have not allowed you to have many things you wanted, but their denial was a blessing, not a curse. I have showered My gifts on you—in part, because of the frailty and difficulty of your nature. The abundance of My mercy toward you is better than the abundance you could have gathered with a more attractive and winsome nature. The brokenness you have carried inside is a necessary part of this gift, so that it may yet bear the fruit and harvest I intend for it. In the meantime, let it all work its work in your soul and give thanks!

August Twenty–sixth

Thy righteousness is like the great mountains; Thy judgments are a great deep.

Psalm 36:6

The depths of My love you cannot know as long as you cling to your old life. There are many overt and subtle ways of clinging. You are loathe to give up the little comforts and satisfactions, fleeting though they be. But they exact a price all out of keeping with their reward. You must become more aware of their temptation, for you too easily give in without a thought of their real and destructive nature. Your mind is a mine field. Your thoughts are weapons in the hand of the adversary, and you do not even recognize them as such. I do not want you to become super-spiritual and unnatural. I do not call you to weirdness. Rather to awareness—full consciousness of the reality of the warfare which is in your life. If you will choose this, I will help you. If you refuse it, you will suffer great loss.

August Twenty–seventh

The Lord hath been mindful of us: He will bless us; He will bless the house of Israel; He will bless the house of Aaron. He will bless them that fear the Lord, both small and great.

Psalm 115:12,13

Your knowledge of Me is grounded in My dealings with you. I am mindful of you, even when you are not mindful of Me. I am at work in the circumstances and consciences of those for whom you pray. You do not yet realize the power of prayer nor its place in My universe. You have only "tapped the surface" of prayer as yet. But I give you indications, "earnests," to show that I am in your prayers and that I move you to pray. As you obey My Spirit you come to a fuller, firmer knowledge of Me, and are blessed. I am ever mindful of you, My child.

August Twenty–eighth

Therefore with joy shall ye draw water out of the wells of salvation.
Isaiah 12:3

Draw near to Me, My child, and I will not fail to draw near to you. You never seek Me in vain, no matter what your feelings tell you. I, the Lord, change not. My face is ever toward you for good even when you are least aware of it.

Out of the well of salvation comes the water of life. Drink deeply of this life-giving Spirit, My child, that you may be a conveyor of that water to others. Look for opportunities to witness to My goodness to others, and deny the negative spirit.

August Twenty–ninth

But I fear, lest by any means, as the serpent beguiled Eve through his subtlety, so your minds should be corrupted from the simplicity that is in Christ.
II Corinthians 11:3

I am nearer than breathing, closer than hands and feet. I am *within*, though you know it not. When you listen, My child, listen within, where Spirit communes with spirit. Do not doubt and mistrust what you hear. Doubt drives a wedge between your spirit and Mine. It is the work of the adversary of your soul, to prevent you from entering into the fullness of your birthright. "The simplicity that is in Christ" is here—Christ in you, the hope of glory.

August Thirtieth

. . . my strength is made perfect in weakness.

II Corinthians 12:9

My dear child, calm yourself at My breast. Let your faint knowledge of Me give you strength for your needs. I am enough—sufficient for any circumstance you are called to face. There is *always* within the circumstance grace to bear it and a way through.

I have not called you to walk a blind path, even though the future is unknown to you. I have called you to walk *with* Me, and I tell you again, I am enough—sufficient for any circumstance you are called to face. No exceptions!

August Thirty–first

Thou hast set my feet in a large room.

Psalm 31:8

A certain man lived in a large, beautiful mansion. It was made of stone and was built to last indefinitely. The house was occupied by a suitable staff of servants, ready to supply his every need. From time to time people would pass by and comment on the beauty and stability of the house, and would wonder what it was like inside. One thing they noticed: a small, rather unsightly path made its way across the lawn to a back servants' entrance. And the man, the owner, always approached his home via this path and through this door. What others did not know was that the man, the owner of this large, beautiful stone mansion, lived in one small servant's room in the back of the house. It had been so long since he even visited the other rooms that he couldn't remember what they looked like, and felt no sense of identity as their owner. Nor did he call on his servants to help him. Instead, he went in and out, afraid of losing his little servant's room, and angry that he found life so dull and uninteresting. He was very conscious of his aches and pains, his changing moods, and often retired to his room hurt and angry at what others said or thought.

Let those hear who have ears to hear. . . .

About Paraclete Press

Who We Are

Paraclete Press is an ecumenical publisher of books and recordings on Christian spirituality. Our publishing represents a full expression of Christian belief and practice—from Catholic to Evangelical, from Protestant to Orthodox.

Paraclete Press is the publishing arm of the Community of Jesus, an ecumenical monastic community in the Benedictine tradition. As such, we are uniquely positioned in the marketplace without connection to a large corporation and with informal relationships to many branches and denominations of faith.

We like it best when people buy our books from booksellers, our partners in successfully reaching as wide an audience as possible.

What We Are Doing
Books

Paraclete Press publishes books that show the richness and depth of what it means to be Christian. Although Benedictine spirituality is at the heart of all that we do, we publish books that reflect the Christian experience across many cultures, time periods, and houses of worship.

We publish books that nourish the vibrant life of the church and its people—books about spiritual practice, formation, history, ideas, and customs.

We have several different series of books within Paraclete Press, including the best-selling Living Library series of modernized classic texts; A Voice from the Monastery—giving voice to men and women monastics about what it means to live a spiritual life today; award-winning literary faith fiction; and books that explore Judaism and Islam and discover how these faiths inform Christian thought and practice.

Recordings

From Gregorian chant to contemporary American choral works, our music recordings celebrate the richness of sacred choral music through the centuries. Paraclete is proud to distribute the recordings of the internationally acclaimed choir Gloriæ Dei Cantores, who have been praised for their "rapt and fathomless spiritual intensity" by *American Record Guide,* and the Gloriæ Dei Cantores Schola, which specializes in the study and performance of Gregorian chant. Paraclete is also the exclusive North American distributor of the recordings of the Monastic Choir of St. Peter's Abbey in Solesmes, France, long considered to be a leading authority on Gregorian chant performance.

Learn more about us at our Web site:
www.paracletepress.com, or call us toll-free at
800-451-5006.

Must-have Companions on Your Journey to Wholeness

Your Whole Life Journal
Record your progress with this convenient, inspirational, spiral-bound journal designed for twelve weeks of your 3D journey.
$14.95

Your Whole Life Inspirational CD
Get inspired each morning by a message from Carol Showalter— one for each of the twelve weeks. This engaging, 36-minute CD is also ideal for playing aloud at your weekly meetings.
$16.95

The 3D Prayer Card
"Dear Lord, This is a new day . . ."
A personal prayer by Carol Showalter, beautifully designed and laminated.

Available in packs of 10
$4.95/pack

THE 3D PLAN

For more information, go to the 3D website,
www.3DYourWholeLife.com, or call 1-800-451-5006